The Suicide Epidemic

Bradley Steffens

ReferencePoint Press®

San Diego, CA

© 2020 ReferencePoint Press, Inc.
Printed in the United States

For more information, contact:
ReferencePoint Press, Inc.
PO Box 27779
San Diego, CA 92198
www.ReferencePointPress.com

LIBRARY OF CONGRESS CATALOGING-IN-PUBLICATION DATA

Name: Steffens, Bradley, 1955– author.
Title: The Suicide Epidemic/by Bradley Steffens.
Description: San Diego, CA: ReferencePoint Press, Inc., 2020. | Includes
bibliographical references and index.
Identifiers: LCCN 2019014310 (print) | LCCN 2019016156 (ebook) | ISBN
9781682827420 (eBook) | ISBN 9781682827413 (hardback)
Subjects: LCSH: Suicide—United States—Juvenile literature. |
Suicide—United States—Prevention—Juvenile literature.
Classification: LCC HV6548.U5 (ebook) | LCC HV6548.U5 S74 2020 (print) | DDC
362.280973—dc23
LC record available at https://lccn.loc.gov/2019014310

Contents

The Recent Surge in Suicides

Celebrities make news, and celebrity deaths make even bigger news. So when renowned chef Anthony Bourdain, host of CNN's *Anthony Bourdain: Parts Unknown* television program, and Kate Spade, fashion designer and founder of Kate Spade New York, died three days apart in June 2018, their deaths dominated the headlines for days. Adding to the shock and grief of their families, friends, and fans was the manner in which Bourdain and Spade had died: both had taken their own lives. The public wondered why two people who seemed to have everything going for them—wealth, fame, and the admiration of their peers—would intentionally end their lives. It seemed so senseless. In the days and weeks that followed, details about the suicides emerged. According to her family, Spade had been battling anxiety and depression for years. People close to Bourdain say he was struggling with relationship problems.

The same week that Spade and Bourdain put suicide in the spotlight, the Centers for Disease Control and Prevention (CDC) released a major report on suicide in the United States. The CDC found that the US suicide rate had increased among all age groups younger than seventy-five years. "These findings are disturbing," says Anne Schuchat, the CDC's principal deputy director.

> And these statistics don't begin to reveal the emotional, social and financial toll that suicide exacts on individuals, families and communities who are left devastated. Many have lost friends, neighbors and family members to suicide or have loved ones who have considered or attempted it.[1]

The deaths of celebrities Kate Spade and Anthony Bourdain by suicide seemed particularly senseless, since both appeared to have everything going for them.

One Act, Multiple Causes

One of the most surprising findings of the CDC was that fewer than half of the people who died by suicide had a known mental health condition. For years, mental health professionals had said that 90 percent of suicides are related to mental illness. The CDC found that the actual number of suicides with a diagnosed mental illness was about half that—46 percent. The other 54 percent were people who did not have a mental health condition but were struggling with relationship problems, personal losses, or other life stressors.

The CDC pointed out that both those with a diagnosed mental condition and those without one were almost always facing several problems at once. Rarely is there only one factor behind a suicide. For example, a large number of suicides occur among older people who have been diagnosed with a serious disease. They might be depressed because of the state of their health, in physical pain, and coping with the recent loss of a spouse, all at the same time. Add the use of drugs or alcohol, and that person might attempt suicide. This is just one example, however. Similar combinations can be present in any age group—from pre-teens on up. "Suicide, like other human behaviors, has no single determining cause," states the CDC. "Instead, suicide occurs in response to multiple biological, psychological, interpersonal, environmental and societal influences that interact with one another, often over time."[2]

> "Suicide, like other human behaviors, has no single determining cause. Instead, suicide occurs in response to multiple biological, psychological, interpersonal, environmental and societal influences that interact with one another, often over time."[2]
>
> —The CDC

The fact that suicide has no single cause and no simple solution is one of the reasons the rate of suicide continues to rise. In 2017 a total of 47,173 Americans took their own lives, an increase of more than 2,000 suicides over the year before. Suicide is the second-leading cause of death among those aged ten to thirty-four (behind only accidental death) and the fourth-leading cause among those aged thirty-five to fifty-four. Overall, suicide is the tenth-leading cause of death in the United States. "Suicide takes more [firemen] than fire, more police than crime, more lives than car accidents,"[3] says the Columbia Lighthouse Project, a nonprofit organization dedicated to suicide research and prevention.

Widespread Impact

Suicide is an individual act that affects an entire community. According to the CDC, there are six to thirty-two survivors—defined as close friends and family members—for every suicide. That means as many as 1.5 million people were suicide survivors in 2017 alone. These people struggle with immeasurable pain as they cope with the loss of a loved one. But the trauma does not end with them. It ripples outward, affecting an average of 425 people who knew the individual through work, school, church, and other activities, according to a study by the CDC. About half of all American adults have known at least one person who died by suicide, according to a 2016 study by researchers at the University of Kentucky. And the circle widens every year.

Some of those who have lost loved ones to suicide have gone on to devote their lives to suicide prevention, often with the hope that if they could prevent one person from taking his or her life—and spare even one other family the pain they have experienced—their efforts would be worthwhile. Their aspirations reflect the most tragic, frustrating, and yet hopeful aspect of suicide: It is preventable. It is not a disease. It does not emerge from the genes, like some forms of cancer. It is not transmitted by a virus, a pathogen-carrying insect, or unsanitary food or water. "Suicide is preventable," says Schuchat. "That's why it's so important to understand the range of factors and circumstances that contribute to suicide risk, including relationship problems, substance misuse, physical and mental health conditions, job issues, financial troubles, and legal problems."[4] One does not have to be a doctor to recognize the warning signs of suicide or to offer help. Anyone can help save a life and contain the deadly epidemic.

> "Suicide is preventable. That's why it's so important to understand the range of factors and circumstances that contribute to suicide risk."[4]
>
> —Anne Schuchat, principal deputy director of the CDC

Chapter 1

A Disturbing Trend

Solomon Thomas is a defensive end for the San Francisco 49ers of the National Football League. It is a particularly tough position to play, requiring the player to overpower or outmaneuver an offensive blocker on nearly every play. "There's a saying that you have to be a little mean to play football," says Thomas.

> One day when I was at practice at Stanford [University, where Thomas played college football], my D-line [defensive line] coach asked where I got my meanness. I stopped and thought for a minute, and told him that, honestly, I got beat up too many times by my sister![5]

When they were kids, Solomon and his older sister, Ella, would wrestle. Despite Solomon's size—close to 200 pounds (91 kg) in third grade—Ella would always get the better of him.

Ella was an inspiration for more than Solomon's toughness, however. She was also an excellent student and accomplished athlete. But when Ella was in college, she was sexually assaulted—a fact that she kept from her family for three years. She began to suffer from depression. In 2017 she started seeing a therapist and taking anxiety medication. "She would seem happy, and things would be going well with friends and at work. But then out of the blue she would get so sad again," recalls Solomon. On January 23, 2018, Ella took her life. Solomon remembers:

> My dad called and told me what happened. I was at home alone. I collapsed and fell to the ground, screaming and crying. . . . My mom was at Ella's friend's house, where she died. My dad didn't want me to go, but I had to. I drove

over there, hoping and praying it wasn't true. But when I saw red and blue lights flashing, I knew. I saw my mom crying and walked over to her. Then we just hugged and cried and screamed together.[6]

Increasing Rates of Suicide

It is a scene that is playing out in increasing numbers all across the United States. From 1999 through 2017, the US suicide rate increased 33 percent, from 10.5 to 14.0 per 100,000 population, according to a 2018 report by the CDC. Since 2006, suicide rates have risen by 2 percent per year.

Ella Thomas's suicide was part of another disturbing trend. The rate of suicide for women grew by a staggering 50 percent from 2000 to 2016, according to the CDC. The rate for men increased 21 percent over the same period. In part this is because fewer women than men commit suicide, so a modest increase in raw numbers translates into a large increase in percentage. In 2000 the ratio of male-to-female suicide rates was 4.4 men to 1 woman. But the gap is narrowing. In 2016 it was 3.6 men to 1 woman.

> "My dad called and told me what happened. I was at home alone. I collapsed and fell to the ground, screaming and crying."[6]
>
> —Solomon Thomas, suicide survivor

The Trauma of War

Suicide rates have risen among all races, ages, and genders, but they have risen more dramatically in some populations than others. For example, a 2016 study by the US Department of Veterans Affairs (VA) found that the suicide rate among veterans had increased 35 percent since 2001—two percentage points higher than the national average. The increase among female veterans was a mind-boggling 85 percent. The rate of veterans' suicides was already higher than the general population's before the increase. As a result, veterans die by suicide at more than 1.5 times the rate of nonveterans.

Since 2001 the United States has been involved in wars in Afghanistan, Iraq, and Syria, leaving many veterans with post-traumatic stress disorder (PTSD) and greater risk for suicide. "War inflicts permanent psychic scars on survivors," says Danny O'Neel, a US Army veteran who served in Iraq. "That trauma can be more deadly than war itself. More of my brothers from that deployment have died from suicide than combat: Nine were killed in Iraq; 15 have killed themselves back at home."[7]

O'Neel was nearly one of them. "On July 14, 2012, drowning in grief and guilt, I tried to kill myself," he remembers. "Like so many veterans, I had found civilian life desperately difficult. War had drained me of joy. The sights, sounds and smells of the battlefield had been relentlessly looping in my head. The suffering seemed endless. And so, thinking there were no other options of escape, I turned to suicide."[8] After surviving his suicide attempt, O'Neel dedicated his life to helping other veterans. He founded an organization, the Independence Fund, that has teamed up with the VA to provide mental health training services for vets and their families.

Active duty military personnel also have a higher suicide rate than the general population: 17 per 100,000, compared with 14 per 100,000 for the general population. As with veterans, the trauma of combat often contributes to suicidal thoughts. "The real problem is the culture in the military that says suck it up and drive on, and if you can't suck it up and drive on, then you're weak and you have no place here," says Ellen Haring, a retired

> "War inflicts permanent psychic scars on survivors. That trauma can be more deadly than war itself. More of my brothers from that deployment have died from suicide than combat."[7]
>
> —Danny O'Neel, a US Army veteran who served in Iraq

The suicide rate among military veterans is 1.5 times higher than among nonveterans.

army colonel and now the director of programs and research at the Service Women's Action Network, a nonprofit organization that advocates for active duty and veteran servicewomen. "Until we change our culture to say, hey, it's actually strong to be able to recognize your own needs, that that's not a weakness, to be introspective, then we're going to continue to see this problem."[9]

An Occupational Hazard

The military is not the only profession with a high suicide risk. A November 2018 study by the CDC found that the suicide rate among the US working-age population increased 34 percent from 2000 to 2016, one percentage point more than the rate for the general population. But some professions have much higher rates than the US average. For example, men working in the construction and mining and petroleum extraction industry occupational group have a suicide rate of 53.2 per 100,000 population, or 2.4 times the rate of all men and almost four times the national rate of men and women combined. This could be because men in those industries are often working far from population centers and might not have suicide counseling readily available. They also might have the warrior mentality that Haring describes among members of the military, namely that "real" men are not supposed to complain about the difficulty of their jobs or seek help for emotional problems.

For women, the suicide rate is highest in those industries with different kinds of pressures, those of meeting aggressive goals and deadlines: the media and the arts, design, entertainment, and sports. The suicide rate among females in the media is 15.6 per 100,000, or about 2.5 times higher than the rate for the general female population. Suicide in the category of arts, design, entertainment, and sports is 11.7 per 100,000, or about twice the rate for women generally. These industries also saw the greatest increase in the suicide rate for men from 2012 to 2015—a 47 percent increase. The industry with the greatest increase for women in the same time period was food preparation and serving, with a 54 percent increase.

Identifying which populations are at greatest risk is a standard approach of public health professionals. "Knowing who is at greater risk for suicide can help save lives through focused prevention efforts,"[10] says Debra Houry, director of the CDC's National Center for Injury Prevention and Control.

Dangers in the Medical Field

Some of the occupations with high suicide rates are surprising. For example, a December 2018 study by the CDC found that female veterinarians were 3.5 times as likely to die from suicide as the general population, while male veterinarians were only 2.1 times as likely. The higher suicide rate for female veterinarians is particularly concerning because more than 60 percent of US veterinarians are women.

Veterinarians who treat small animals, including dogs and cats, were at greater risk of suicide than those treating larger ani-

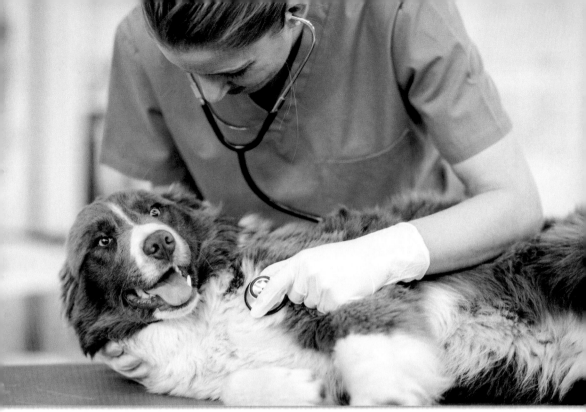

According to the CDC, female veterinarians are 3.5 times as likely to die from suicide as the general population.

mals, including horses and cattle; 75 percent of the veterinarians who died by suicide worked in a small animal practice. One of the possible reasons for this is the greater emotional demands of caring for beloved family pets compared with caring for farm animals. But as with suicide in general, there is no single cause for the high rate of suicide among veterinarians. The researchers cite the profession's long work hours, work overload, client expectations and complaints, euthanasia procedures, and poor work-life balance as some of the risk factors. "This study shines a light on a complex issue in this profession," says CDC director Robert R. Redfield. "Using this knowledge, we can work together to reduce the number of suicides among veterinarians."[11]

The study also identified another contributing factor to veterinarian suicides: access to drugs used to euthanize animals and the knowledge to calculate a dose that would kill a person. The study found that 37 percent of suicide deaths among veterinarians

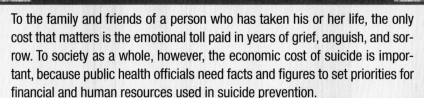

The Economic Cost of Suicide

To the family and friends of a person who has taken his or her life, the only cost that matters is the emotional toll paid in years of grief, anguish, and sorrow. To society as a whole, however, the economic cost of suicide is important, because public health officials need facts and figures to set priorities for financial and human resources used in suicide prevention.

Fatal and nonfatal suicide attempts result in two kinds of costs: direct and indirect. Direct costs are related to injury treatment. They include costs for medical care, especially emergency departments and inpatient hospitalization; ambulance transport; investigations by medical examiners or coroners; doctors' care; and follow-up care. Indirect costs are mainly losses in productivity from premature death or lost time from injuries. These include salaries, fringe benefits, and the value of household productivity lost due to suicide or reduced by suicide attempt.

Researchers at the Heller School for Social Policy and Management at Brandeis University in Massachusetts find that the average cost of one suicide is $1.3 millon. More than 97 percent of the cost is due to the lost contributions in productive labor that the people who took their lives otherwise would have made at work and at home. The remaining 3 percent is due to costs associated with medical treatment. Accounting for some underreporting of suicides, the total cost of suicides and suicide attempts was $93.5 billion a year. On the basis of these figures, the researchers estimate that every $1.00 spent on suicide prevention would save $2.50 in the cost of suicides.

were caused by pharmaceutical poisoning. For female veterinarians, the rate was even higher at 64 percent.

Doctors who treat people also have higher rates of suicide than the general population. The American Foundation for Suicide Prevention reports that the suicide rate among female physicians is 2.27 times greater than it is among the general female population, and that of male physicians is 1.41 times higher than that of the general male population. Dentists, anesthetists, and other health professionals also have elevated suicide risks.

One of those was Richard Harding, an anesthetist and intensivist (a specialist in the care of critically ill patients). After a fine career, a complaint was made against him, and he became depressed while the charges were being investigated. "Although the complaint was thrown out in due course, as we expected it to be, it took five months," remembers his wife, Kate, who is a doctor. "The strain this put him under was immense." After Richard was cleared of any wrongdoing, the family moved to New Zealand to start over, but Richard's depression lingered. "This time, the medication didn't work; in fact, it may have made things worse," says Kate. "Insomnia was a central feature, worsened by the frequency of his night-time call-outs, although he enjoyed his job and continued to perform well at work."[12] Kate remembers that her husband kept saying, "I don't think I will ever be the same person again."[13] She believes he became frustrated with the failure of the drugs and the various referrals and delays in treatment that he received. "Richard lost patience with the process and took matters into his own hands," says Kate. While she was out walking the dog with her daughter, Richard killed himself at home. "I am still in a state of disbelief much of the time," says Kate. "To say I feel overwhelmed by guilt and shame is an understatement. As his wife and as a doctor, I am appalled that I let him go this way. The phrase 'I have lost my husband' could not be more accurate—it feels like carelessness to me, like he slipped through my fingers while I looked the other way. I went on a walk; I returned to find my husband dead."[14]

> "To say I feel overwhelmed by guilt and shame is an understatement."[14]
>
> —Kate Harding, suicide survivor

High-Risk Populations

Professions are only one risk factor that public health officials look at when assessing how best to address an epidemic. Age, race, and gender can also play a part. Richard Harding, a white male aged forty-seven, was in the three highest risk groups. Men make up 49 percent of the US population but 77 percent of US suicides.

The suicide rate for men is 3.5 times higher than for women—21.8 per 100,000 population for men and 6.2 for women.

In addition, non-Hispanic whites make up about 63 percent of the US population but 81 percent of US suicides. The suicide rate among non-Hispanic whites of both sexes is 21.8 per 100,000, the highest of all race categories tracked by the CDC. Non-Hispanic American Indians or Alaska Natives are not far behind, with a suicide rate of 21.4 for both sexes. No other racial group reaches a double-digit suicide rate per 100,000 population, with Asians and Pacific Islanders at 7.0, non-Hispanic blacks at 6.4, and Hispanics at 6.0.

Suicide risk also increases by age, up to age fifty-four. The age group of forty-four to fifty-four—the group Harding was in—has the highest rate, 19.7 per 100,000 population, which is about 40

Middle-aged men are particularly at risk of dying by suicide.

Underreporting of Suicide

In 2018 the CDC announced that the US suicide rate was at its highest point in at least fifty years. It is one of only three causes of death that is increasing in the United States—with drug overdose and dementia being the other two. Some experts believe the suicide situation is even worse than the CDC reports. They point out that, like suicide, drug overdoses are often related to depression, loss, or physical or sexual abuse. It is possible and even likely that many drug overdoses are in fact suicides. "It is likely that under-reporting and misclassification are greater problems for suicide than for most other causes of death," states the World Health Organization, an agency within the United Nations.

The same is true for solo traffic fatalities. Researchers believe that some traffic deaths, especially those involving a solo driver in a single car, are in fact suicides that only look like accidents. The person taking his or her life might disguise a suicide out of guilt or so that the suicide's survivors can collect life insurance benefits, since most life insurance companies do not pay a death benefit if a life insurance policy is purchased within two years prior to a suicide.

World Health Organization, "Suicide," August 24, 2018. www.who.int.

percent higher than the national average. The rates go down again after age fifty-four and start to rise again after age seventy-five.

Some smaller populations have especially high risks of suicide. According to a January 2019 report from the CDC, 34.6 percent of transgender youths—those whose gender identity does not align with their biological sex—reported having attempted suicide in the previous twelve months. Transgender youths make up about 2 percent of the US high school population. Thirty-five percent of these students report being bullied at school, and 27 percent say they feel unsafe at school or traveling to or from campus. "Given that violence victimization is a documented risk factor for substance use and suicide risk, implementation of interventions focused on reducing the victimization of transgender adolescents

> "There is never one reason for someone to take their life; suicide is a very unfortunate, tragic outcome of a complex set of circumstances."[16]
>
> —Gaurav Chawla, chief medical officer at Providence Behavioral Health Hospital

might be a key strategy for improving overall health,"[15] state researchers.

The suicide epidemic is different from other types of epidemic. It is not geographically localized, the way the outbreak of a deadly virus might be. It is not confined to one age group, the way dementia is to elderly adults. It is not linked to lifestyle, as type 2 diabetes is to obesity or certain cancers are to tobacco use. Different factors seem to be at work in different groups, and these factors usually combine with other conditions such as drug or alcohol use, impulsivity, or depression to trigger a suicide attempt. "Suicide is a confluence of circumstances that lead one to conclude that they're trapped in a hopeless circumstance, sometimes without purpose, in a painful existence from which there is no other way out," says Gaurav Chawla, chief medical officer at Providence Behavioral Health Hospital in Holyoke, Massachusetts. "There is never one reason for someone to take their life; suicide is a very unfortunate, tragic outcome of a complex set of circumstances."[16]

Chapter 2

The Causes of Suicide

To prevent suicide—or any epidemic—public health officials need to understand the causes behind it. This is extremely difficult to do in the case of suicide, for three reasons. First, there is no single root cause. Second, the various factors that may contribute to suicide are experienced by many people and are not by themselves life threatening. And third, the contributing factors can change over the course of a lifetime. This makes the prediction of who is at risk of suicide extremely difficult.

Mental Illness

Almost half of those who die of suicide (46 percent) have been diagnosed with some form of mental illness before they take their lives. Mental illnesses are health conditions involving significant changes in emotion, thinking, or behavior. These conditions are often associated with problems functioning in social settings, at work or school, or during family activities. Mental illness conditions are surprisingly common. According to the American Psychiatric Association, nearly one in five US adults—some 48 million people—experience some form of mental illness in a given year. Mental illness is treatable. "The vast majority of individuals with mental illness continue to function in their daily lives,"[17] states the association.

According to a 2018 study by the CDC, depression is the most common disorder among those suicides in which the person had a diagnosed mental condition, present in 75 percent of such suicides. Depression is not just feeling sad, which is a normal human emotion that everyone experiences from time to time. Sadness usually passes in a few days. Depression, also known as major depressive disorder, is different.

It has long-lasting symptoms that can include overwhelming sadness, low energy, loss of appetite, and a lack of interest in things that a person normally enjoys. "When worthlessness, hopelessness, and pervasive sadness exist, a person's meaning for living plummets, increasing their risk of suicide,"[18] says Lena Franklin, a psychotherapist in Atlanta, Georgia.

Often, depression is the result of an imbalance of the natural chemicals in the brain known as neurotransmitters. These chemicals allow nerve cells in the brain, known as neurons, to transmit chemical messages to one another. A shortage of the chemical can prevent nerve messages from being passed along properly. This can affect a person's mood and outlook, resulting in depression. The chemical and physical basis of depression means that the illness is involuntary, just like neurological illnesses such as Parkinson's disease and Alzheimer's disease. The chemical basis of depression also means that it is treatable. Depression is often treated with medications that restore a balance of the chemicals.

> "When worthlessness, hopelessness, and pervasive sadness exist, a person's meaning for living plummets, increasing their risk of suicide."[18]
>
> —Lena Franklin, a psychotherapist in Atlanta, Georgia

Depression is a risk factor for suicide because the chemical imbalance can keep the depressed person from feeling like things can get better. Suicide Awareness Voices of Education explains:

Many people who suffer from depression report feeling as though they've lost the ability to imagine a happy future, or remember a happy past. Often they don't realize they're suffering from a treatable illness, and seeking help may not even enter their mind. Emotions and even physical pain can become unbearable. They don't want to die, but it's the only way they feel their pain will end. It is a truly irrational choice.[19]

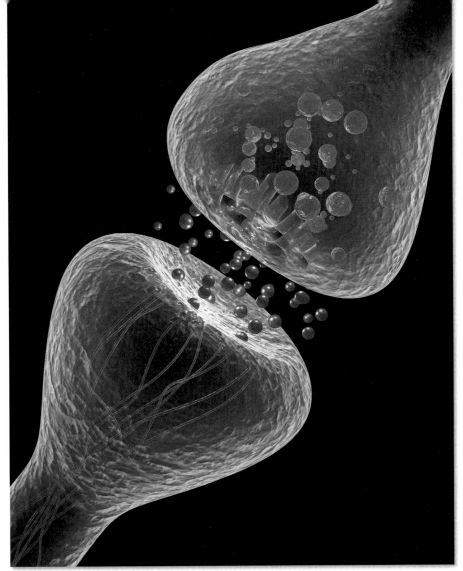

An imbalance of neurotransmitters (depicted here as pink spheres passing from one nerve cell to another) can cause mood disorders such as depression, which is a known risk factor for suicide.

Millions of Americans experience depression each year, but only a small percentage of them go on to commit suicide. According to the CDC, an estimated 16.2 million adults in the United States had at least one major depressive episode in 2016. This number represents 6.7 percent of all US adults. A significant number of these, about one-third, think about suicide, a process known as suicide ideation. The number who die by suicide is much smaller, only about 4 percent. The percentage is so small

A Strongman Battles Suicidal Thoughts

Craig Toley, an athlete who competes in strongman events, became suicidal after learning he had cancer. "I've always been a mentally strong guy, but when cancer came, it broke me," says Toley.

Toley was diagnosed with thyroid cancer at age twenty-nine. Surgeons removed his thyroid, and he received radiation treatment. "When my treatment was nearing its end, I spiralled into a dark depression that I kept from everyone around me," he remembers. "I was in a dark place mentally. I would have visions where I imagined my own death, but I didn't realise that these were suicidal thoughts." He organized a charity strongman competition so he would have something to focus on other than his health, but it failed to have the desired effect. In fact, the depression worsened.

Finally, Toley went to see a counselor. "I went in and cried my eyes out. The counselor wanted to put me on antidepressants as she believed I was suicidal. Hearing someone say that made me realise how serious it was," he says. Toley did not go on the medication, but after each therapy session he felt a little better. "If I was able to go back in time and speak to myself when I was diagnosed, I would encourage myself to cry," says Toley. "Cry for as long as I need to cry and to talk, talk to my family, talk to my friends and not to hold onto the emotion that almost pushed me to the edge."

Craig Toley, "My Cancer Diagnosis Made Me Suicidal," Metro, January 22, 2019. https://metro.co.uk.

that depression by itself is not considered a predictor of suicide. "Depression predicts suicide ideation, but not suicide plans or attempts among those with ideation,"[20] write researchers at Harvard University Medical School.

The risk of attempting suicide increases when a person has depression combined with a disorder characterized by anxiety or agitation, such as PTSD, or with poor impulse control, such as conduct disorder. The same is true when depression is combined with drug or alcohol abuse. A third of all completed suicides involve heavy use of alcohol.

Serious Mental Illnesses

According to the CDC, about 10 percent of suicides in which the person had previously been diagnosed with a mental illness involve what is termed a "serious" mental illness. A serious mental illness is one that substantially interferes with or limits major life activities. Examples include bipolar disorder, depressive psychosis, and schizophrenia. According to the CDC, one in twenty-four US adults (4.1 percent) has a serious mental illness. These numbers are smaller than for depression, but the suicide rates for people with these mental illnesses are much higher. A 2018 study published in the medical journal *Psychiatric Services* found that people with bipolar disorder are twenty-three times more likely to take their lives using means other than firearms and eight times more likely to take their lives using firearms than the general population. People with schizophrenia are twenty-four times more likely to take their lives using means other than firearms and ten times more likely to take their lives with firearms.

Lisa Abramson, a new mom in San Francisco, was nearly one of those suicides. In 2014 Abramson gave birth to her first child, Lucy. At first, motherhood was as wonderful as Abramson had imagined it would be. After one week, however, Lucy began losing weight. The pediatrician told Abramson, who was breast-feeding, to feed the baby every two hours. Getting little sleep and worrying about the baby, Abramson began to have negative thoughts about herself. "It weighed on me as, 'I've failed as a mom. I can't feed my child,'" she says. For a brief escape, Abramson took a spin class at the local gym. After ten minutes she had to leave. "The noises and intense volume of the spin class [were] really alarming to me," says Abramson. "It felt like the walls were talking to me." A couple of weeks later, she looked outside her window and saw police helicopters circling her apartment building. "There were snipers on the roof. There were spy cams in our bedroom. And everyone was watching me. And my cellphone was, like, giving me weird messages,"[21] she says.

Abramson believed the police were going to arrest her. When she woke up the next morning and was still at home, she assumed the police had taken her nanny instead. She felt that was unfair, and she told her husband that to fix the situation, she would take her life by jumping off the Golden Gate Bridge. Her husband, David, realized what was happening. There were no helicopters, no snipers, and no spy cameras—his wife was hallucinating. David told Lisa that he would take her to the police, but he took her to a psychiatric hospital instead.

Abramson's doctors diagnosed her with postpartum (after giving birth) psychosis, a form of depressive psychosis that studies show might affect as many as two out of every one thousand new mothers. Like other depressive orders, postpartum depressive psychosis can be caused by changes in the natural chemicals in the body. After childbirth, the levels of the hormones estrogen and progesterone in the mother's body can drop dramatically, triggering changes in mood. Other hormones produced by the thyroid gland may also drop sharply, leaving the new mother feeling tired, sluggish, and depressed.

Eventually, Abramson recovered. She and her husband even decided to have a second child. Abramson did not have depressive psychosis after the birth of her second daughter, Vivian, in part because she took many precautions, including getting enough sleep. "We've got so many messages of just self-sacrifice," says Abramson. "'Do anything for your kids.' 'Drop everything. That's what it means to be a good mom.' And for me, that's not what made me a good mom. That's what made me fall apart."[22]

Suicide Without Diagnosed Mental Illness

Just as the metabolic changes from giving birth can leave a person feeling overwhelmed and hopeless, so too can other major life changes and problems. According to a 2018 CDC study, the leading factors contributing to suicide include relationship problems, personal crises, substance abuse, and health problems. Coping with any one circumstance is usually manage-

Factors That Contribute to Suicide

Many factors contribute to suicide. According to the Centers for Disease Control and Prevention, relationship problems are at the top of the list. The next most common factor is when someone experiences a personal crisis. Substance abuse is the third most common factor. In some instances, multiple factors and/or mental illness are tied to a person's decision to commit suicide.

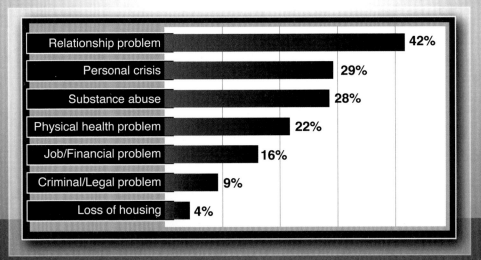

Relationship problem	42%
Personal crisis	29%
Substance abuse	28%
Physical health problem	22%
Job/Financial problem	16%
Criminal/Legal problem	9%
Loss of housing	4%

Source: Centers for Disease Control and Prevention, "Suicide Rising Across the US," June 2018. www.cdc.gov.

able, but when two or three problems converge at once, people can begin to feel their problems are insurmountable. They might begin to think about suicide as the only solution and then act on those thoughts.

In that study, the CDC found, for instance, that a physical health problem was a factor in 22 percent of suicides. Among those are people diagnosed with cancer. A 2019 study by researchers at the Penn State University College of Medicine finds that people with cancer are more than four times more likely to die of suicide than those without cancer. This rate has doubled since 2002, when cancer patients had a twofold risk of suicide. Since cancer is the leading cause of death in the United States, many people believe that being diagnosed with it is a death sentence. In addition, cancer treatment is often lengthy and difficult.

Roy B. Sessions, a cancer surgeon who has had several of his patients commit suicide, says:

> Consider, if you will, the enormity of what the cancer patient faces—the forces of depression/anxiety, fear, discouragement, concern for financial and family compromise, a desperate search for privacy and dignity, and lastly the avoidance of going through the general misery of the terminal period—all come together in an avalanche of psychic forces. Some patients simply say to themselves, "Who needs all of this?"[23]

The Penn State researchers reviewed the records of more than 8 million patients diagnosed with cancer between 1970 and 2014. The researchers found that the risk of suicide compared with that of the general population is highest in those with cancer of the lung, head and neck, testes, and lymph system (Hodgkin's lymphoma). The risk of suicide was lowest in those with prostate, bladder, and colorectal cancer. The age of the person and the effect of treatment on that person's quality of life also affected the level of suicide risk. "Treatments for some cancers—like leukemia and testicular cancer among adolescents and young adults, for example—can decrease a patient's fertility, and that seems to be one of the risks for suicide in the long term,"[24] says Nicholas Zaorsky, one of the authors of the study.

Bereavement and Suicide

The death of a family member can be so painful that it triggers suicidal thoughts in some survivors. A Swedish study found that people who had experienced the death of a brother or sister were at greater risk of suicide than people who had not experienced the loss of a family member. In women the suicide risk was 1.55 times that of nonbereaved persons. In men it was 1.28 times higher. "This finding might reflect the fact that women place more

The death of a family member can be so painful that it triggers thoughts of suicide in some survivors.

emphasis on social relationships than men do, particularly when it comes to parents and the family," explain the researchers, Mikael Rostila, Jan Saarela, and Ichiro Kawachi. "The loss of a sibling could hence have stronger emotional consequences for women which, in turn, could account for a higher risk of suicide."[25]

The numbers increased for both women and men if the sibling had died from suicide. In such cases the risk was 3.19 times higher among women and 2.44 times higher among men than the non-bereaved population. "Survivors of suicide seem to struggle more with questions of meaning around the death," write the researchers. "Survivors often show higher levels of guilt, blame and responsibility for the death than other mourners."[26]

> "Survivors of suicide seem to struggle more with questions of meaning around the death. Survivors often show higher levels of guilt, blame and responsibility for the death than other mourners."[26]
>
> —Mikael Rostila, Jan Saarela, and Ichiro Kawachi, mental health researchers

A Celebrity Blames American Culture for the High Suicide Rate

Kirsten Powers, a news analyst for CNN, believes the emptiness of American culture is to blame for the high rate of suicide in the United States. Powers herself attempted suicide following the death of her father in 2004. "I couldn't imagine a life without my father and our hours-long conversations about, well, everything," she says. "The pain was debilitating, getting out of bed was an Olympian event, and life was utterly devoid of meaning."

Powers says friends and family had a hard time accepting that she was suicidal because she was "living the dream." But Powers says that success is a double-edged sword. "In many ways achieving all your goals provides the opposite of fulfillment: It lays bare the truth that there is nothing you can purchase, possess or achieve that will make you feel fulfilled over the long term."

The reason for this emptiness, Powers, believes, is that Americans are striving so hard for success that they have lost a sense of connectedness with each other. "We are too busy trying to 'make it' without realizing that once we reach that goal, it won't be enough," she says. In such a society, she says, despair and emotional suffering are "a rational response to a culture that values people based on ever escalating financial and personal achievements." She believes that some people are suicidal because of mental illness. "But most Americans are depressed, anxious or suicidal because something is wrong with our culture, not because something is wrong with them."

Kirsten Powers, "Americans Are Depressed and Suicidal Because Something Is Wrong with Our Culture," *USA Today*, June 9, 2018. www.usatoday.com.

Economics and Suicide

Most researchers search for causes of suicide at the individual level, but some researchers have taken a broader look at things, focusing on the economic hardships that the CDC says are factors in about 20 percent of suicides. For example, economists Anne Case and Angus Deaton found that while life expectancy has been increasing in the United States for the past one hundred years, it has been declining for middle-aged white Americans since 1999.

Among whites aged forty-five to fifty-four, mortality rates increased by 8.9 percent from 1999 to 2013, while death rates among blacks and Hispanics in the same age group decreased. Case and Deaton found that the drop in life expectancy was due mainly to increases in suicide, drug overdose, and alcohol-related liver disease. From 1999 to 2015, deaths by drugs, alcohol, and suicide among men and women aged fifty to fifty-four had more than doubled, from about 35 per 100,000 to more than 80 per 100,000.

Looking deeper, Case and Deaton found the higher death rates were accompanied by lower participation in the workforce, especially among those without a college education. Case and Deaton called these "deaths of despair," because the people without higher education had little hope of finding work in the information economy. "Many more men are finding themselves in a much more hostile labor market with lower wages, lower quality and less permanent jobs," says Deaton. "That's made it harder for them to get married. They don't get to know their own kids. There's a lot of social dysfunction building up over time. There's a sense that these people have lost this sense of status and belonging. And these are classic preconditions for suicide."[27]

> "There's a lot of social dysfunction building up over time. There's a sense that these people have lost this sense of status and belonging. And these are classic preconditions for suicide."[27]
>
> —Angus Deaton, economist

Suicidal thoughts can emerge from many things—chemical imbalances in the body, sudden shocks and upheavals in a person's life, the use of drugs and alcohol, economic hardship, and even the pressures and disconnectedness of an entire culture. But it usually takes a combination of two or more of these factors to push someone into attempting suicide. This makes suicide hard to anticipate in individuals and even harder to curb in a society as large and diverse as that of the United States.

Chapter 3

Teen Suicide

J.C. Ruf was the last person his friends or family expected to take his own life. He had not been diagnosed with a mental condition. He did not abuse drugs or alcohol. He had not cut himself or engaged in other self-harm. A standout pitcher on the Dixie Heights High School baseball team in Dixie Heights, Ohio, Ruf was a kind, compassionate teen who was well liked by classmates. "Whenever I was down or in my own zone, he was always the first person to come to me," says Garrett Vallandingham, who met Ruf in preschool and remained a good friend throughout Ruf's life. "I just felt that I could be open with him. I trust him,"[28] says Vallandingham. Another friend from preschool, Sam Baker, agrees. He says Ruf was "very positive and easy to be around."[29]

Although his parents had divorced, Ruf was surrounded by love, according to his baseball coach, Tom Daria. "He was totally loved. There wasn't violence in the family. There wasn't violence on the baseball field. There was plenty of love going around."[30] Yet on the evening of October 17, 2016, while his mother, Karen, was at a Bible study, J.C. took his grandmother out for dinner. When he returned home, he talked by phone to some of his friends at about 7:30 p.m. No one noticed anything unusual about J.C.'s words or tone of voice. But when his mother returned at around 9:15 p.m., J.C. did not answer her call. She found his lifeless body downstairs, in the laundry. A note on his cell phone made it clear that he had not died accidentally. His death was a suicide.

J.C. Ruf's death is part of an alarming trend. According to a 2018 study by the CDC, the suicide rate for white youth aged ten to seventeen skyrocketed 70 percent from 2006 to 2016. The suicide rate for black children and teens increased even more—77 percent over the same period. The CDC reports that suicide is the second-leading cause of death among youths aged ten to twenty-four. According to the American Foundation for Suicide Prevention, suicide is the leading cause of death among those aged ten to fourteen. "In all my years of community mental health, I've never once been afraid to open my email in the morning," says Tim DeWeese, a mental health professional with the Johnson County Mental Health Center in Kansas. "Today I'm afraid to open my email to see that someone else has committed suicide."[31]

According to the CDC, suicide is the second-leading cause of death among youths.

Impulsive Acts

As with adult suicide, there is no single cause driving the sharp increase in teen suicide. Many of the risk factors for teens are the same as for adults, including mental health problems, easy access to lethal means, alcohol and drug use, and frequent changes in residence that can weaken social connections. In addition, today's teens are facing problems that previous generations did not, including increased pressures from social media, online bullying, and greater numbers of parents with substance abuse problems. Since

A Bullied Teen Takes Her Life

While cyberbullying gets a lot of media attention, serious in-person bullying leads to twice as many teen suicide attempts, according to a 2018 study by researchers at Florida Atlantic University. They found that victims of school bullying were four times as likely to attempt suicide as those who were not bullied, while those who were cyberbullied were two times as likely.

One victim of school bullying was fourteen-year-old Naomi Kempter, a student at Hephzibah Middle School in Hephzibah, Georgia. On May 18, 2018, Kempter took her life when bullying at school became too much for her to handle. "We knew at one point that there was a little bit of trouble at school, but not to the point where we thought something like this would happen," says Kathy Worley, Kempter's grandmother. Only after the teenager's death did the family learn the extent and severity of the bullying. "She had a small journal, and she would write in her journal," says Worley. "It seemed as though whoever was doing the bullying was just really, very harsh."

Kempter's sixteen-year-old friend Americus Fritch teamed up with Bikers Against Bullying to honor Kempter's life and help more victims. "You shouldn't have to be scared of going to school or going to classes every day, and get bullied every day," says Fitch. "If you can't do anything about it, tell your parents. Have your parents do it, but you just have to let somebody know and standup so that you can be heard."

Quoted in Alexa Lightle, "Family, Friends Raise Bullying Awareness After Teen Takes Her Own Life," WRDW-TV News 12 (Augusta, GA), June 20, 2018. www.wrdw.com.

their brains are still developing, teens are not equipped to handle difficulties as well as adults are. "With this population, it's the perfect storm for life to be extra difficult," says Lauren Anderson, executive director of the Josh Anderson Foundation in Vienna, Virginia, a nonprofit suicide prevention organization named after Anderson's seventeen-year-old brother who took his life in 2009. "Based on the development of the brain, they are more inclined to risky behavior, to decide in that moment,"[32] Anderson says.

Thirteen-year-old Cayman Naib of Newton Square, Pennsylvania, was one teenager who decided to take his life on an impulse. On March 4, 2015, Naib received an email from his school notifying him of a failing grade in one of his courses. Distraught, Naib found a gun that belonged to his father. The gun was equipped with a trigger lock, but Naib found a way to discharge the weapon anyway. About half an hour had passed since Naib had received the email. His father, Farid Naib, blames himself for having a gun in the house. "Kids get upset," says Farid. "And they make bad decisions when they're upset. And by having a gun in house that they can access, you give them the ability to make that bad decision permanent."[33]

> "Kids get upset. And they make bad decisions when they're upset. And by having a gun in house that they can access, you give them the ability to make that bad decision permanent."[33]
>
> —Farid Naib, father of Cayman Naib, a teen who took his life at age thirteen

Impulsiveness and easy access to lethal means led another teen to take his life on December 31, 2018. Around 3:15 p.m. on New Year's Eve, fifteen-year-old Devin Hodges was showing a loaded handgun to three of his friends in Lawrenceville, Georgia. The gun accidentally discharged. The bullet struck seventeen-year-old Chad Carless, one of Hodges's friends. The wound was fatal. When police arrived, Hodges panicked. Overcome with remorse and perhaps fearful of what might happen next, Hodges turned the gun on himself and ended his life.

Increasing Risks for Girls

Although boys make up more than 80 percent of the suicides among ten- to twenty-four-year-olds, girls are closing the gap. In 2018 the CDC reported that the suicide rate among teen girls aged ten to fourteen had tripled from 2000 to 2016. Teen girls attempt suicide more than three times as often as boys, and the number of suicide attempts among adolescents is soaring, according to a 2018 study by researchers at Vanderbilt University. The researchers found that the number of adolescents treated in hospitals and emergency rooms for suicidal thoughts and suicide attempts almost tripled from 2008 to 2015, from 0.66 percent in 2008 to 1.82 percent in 2015. More than half of the teen patients were hospitalized overnight, and nearly one in seven required intensive care. The greatest increase in suicide hospitalization was among girls, who made up two-thirds of the cases. The average annual increase in suicide-related hospital visits was 40 percent higher for girls than it was for boys. "What we find nationwide is that over the last decade, the numbers of kids being admitted or seeking help in the emergency department or hospital for suicidal ideation or attempts have dramatically increased,"[34] says Gregory Plemmons, an associate professor of pediatrics at the Monroe Carell Jr. Children's Hospital at Vanderbilt and one of the authors of the study.

The researchers are not sure why teen suicide attempts are increasing at such an explosive rate. "I don't have any one magic answer that explains why we're seeing this," says Plemmons. "We know that anxiety and depression are increasing in young adults as well as adults. I think some people have theorized it's social media maybe playing a role, [in a personal, face-to-face way]."[35]

Social Media and Suicide

One of those who believes social media is contributing to feelings of worthlessness that can lead to suicidal thoughts, especially among girls, is Rachel Simmons, author of *Odd Girl Out: The Hid-*

Some experts believe that social media contributes to feelings of worthlessness that can lead to suicidal thoughts, especially among girls.

den Culture of Aggression in Girls. "It used to be that you didn't know how many friends someone had, or what they were doing after school," Simmons says. "Social media assigns numbers to those things. For the most vulnerable girls, that can be very destabilizing."[36]

Social media can also magnify a teen's awkward moments, turning a private mistake into a public embarrassment. "If something gets said that's hurtful or humiliating, it's not just the kid who said it who knows, it's the entire school or class," explains Marsha Levy-Warren, a clinical psychologist. "In the past, if you made a misstep, it was a limited number of people who would know about it."[37] The pain of such embarrassment can be intense. John Trautwein, the father of Will Trautwein, a fifteen-year-old in Duluth, Georgia, who took his life, believes that the pressures of social media contributed to his son's death. "Every single mistake that Will ever made, there was a fear that it would be on YouTube, on

Snapchat, on Facebook," remembers John. "They know that if they mess up, everyone will know about it by lunchtime. I did not have to deal with that when I was growing up."[38]

Cyberbullying

Today's teens also have to deal with another issue earlier generations did not: cyberbullying. According to the National Center for Telehealth and Technology, cyberbullying refers to when a person is intentionally and repeatedly targeted by another person in the form of threats, harassments, humiliation, or embarrassment via technologies such as email, texting, social networking sites, or instant messaging. Bullying has always existed, but the Internet gives bullies the ability to hide their identities from their victims. This anonymity allows bullies to be even more vicious than they normally would be in face-to-face confrontations. Social media also allows their taunts and humiliations to be seen by far more people.

> "Every single mistake that Will ever made, there was a fear that it would be on YouTube, on Snapchat, on Facebook. They know that if they mess up, everyone will know about it by lunchtime."[38]
>
> —John Trautwein, father of Will Trautwein, who took his life at age fifteen

A 2018 study by the Pew Research Center found that 59 percent of US teens aged thirteen to seventeen have been bullied or harassed online. The survey found that the vast majority of teens (90 percent) believe online harassment is a problem that affects people their age, and 63 percent call it a major problem. A national survey of twelve- to seventeen-year-olds conducted in 2018 by researchers at Florida Atlantic University found that victims of serious cyberbullying were more than two times as likely to attempt suicide as those who were not.

David Molak, a sophomore at Alamo Heights High School in Alamo Heights, Texas, was one such victim of cyberbullying. An

Transgender Teens Face Higher Suicide Risk

A 2019 CDC report had disturbing news about suicidal behavior among transgender youths—those whose gender identity does not align with their biological sex. A team of CDC researchers found that transgender boys (boys who identify as female), who make up about 2 percent of the US high school population, are 2.58 times more likely to feel sad or hopeless than their cisgender peers—boys whose gender identity aligns with their sex. Transgender boys were also 3.95 times as likely to have considered attempting suicide, 3.72 more likely to have made a suicide plan, 6.3 times more likely to have attempted suicide. Cisgender girls were more likely than cisgender boys to have experienced all of these suicidal behaviors, but the rates of transgender boys exceeded those of cisgender girls as well.

One of the reasons that transgender boys have higher rates of suicidal behavior is that they often are on the receiving end of verbal abuse and violence because of their gender identity. Thirty-five percent of these students report being bullied at school, and 27 percent say they feel unsafe at school or traveling to or from campus. "Given that violence victimization is a documented risk factor for substance use and suicide risk, implementation of interventions focused on reducing the victimization of transgender adolescents might be a key strategy for improving overall health," stated the researchers.

Quoted in Michelle M. Johns et al., "Transgender Identity and Experiences of Violence Victimization, Substance Use, Suicide Risk, and Sexual Risk Behaviors Among High School Students—19 States and Large Urban School Districts, 2017," Centers for Disease Control and Prevention, January 25, 2019. www.cdc.gov.

Eagle Scout, an avid San Antonio Spurs fan, and a fitness enthusiast, David had many friends and was dating a girl whom his older brother, Cliff Molak, described as the school's "queen bee." That, according to his tormentors, was the problem. "These people were bashing him for no reason," says Cliff. "He did not do anything to them besides having an attractive girlfriend."[39] The bullies kept up a relentless barrage of insults for three months. David did not keep the bullying to himself. He reported it his family, and his parents took the step of transferring him from Alamo Heights High

School to San Antonio Christian Academy before Christmas 2015. But a physical move is not always enough to escape from bullies in today's interconnected, online world. On January 3, 2016, a group of six to ten unknown phone numbers added David to a group text in which he began receiving comments berating him on his physical appearance. "My first response to him was 'These kids suck, that's really the best insult they can come up with?' but I didn't get the response I wanted. I thought he would laugh but he just stared off into the distance and you could see his pain," remembers Cliff. Later that night or early the next morning, David took his life in the backyard of the family home. "He was just a

Cliff Molak, shown here visiting his brother David's grave, blames cyberbullying for his brother's suicide.

pure-spirited guy," Cliff says. "But, they crushed his spirit and took away his motivation to do anything." Cliff later posted a tribute to his brother on Facebook that went viral: "In today's age, bullies don't push you into lockers, they don't tell their victims to meet them behind the school's dumpster after class, they cower behind user names and fake profiles from miles away constantly berating and abusing good, innocent people."[40]

The Pressures of School

David Molak, Will Trautwein, Devin Hodges, Cayman Naib, and J.C. Ruf all took their lives during the school year. According to the 2018 Vanderbilt University study, this is not a coincidence. The study of those hospital records found that teen suicides were lowest during the summer and highest during the school year. During the eight years included in the study, only 18.5 percent of total annual suicide ideation and suicide attempts occurred during summer months. Peaks were highest in the fall and spring. October accounted for nearly twice as many suicide-related hospital visits as reported in July. The pattern is markedly different from that of adults, for whom July and August are high-risk months. According to Plemmons, performance anxiety or social pressures could be factors.

This was almost certainly the case for Ruf, who hated school, according to his grandmother. In October, the month Ruf took his life, the baseball season had come to an end, and school was all that was left. "October was a down month for him,"[41] says his mother. The pressures of school were obvious in the suicide of Naib, who took his life shortly after receiving a bad report from school.

A 2019 study by the Pew Research Center supports the idea that school is a major pressure for teens. Researchers found that the pressure to get good grades was the leading source of stress for teens aged thirteen to seventeen, with 61 percent saying they personally feel "a lot" of pressure to get good grades, and 27 percent saying they feel "some" pressure to do so. The number of teens who feel a lot of pressure to get good grades is more than double the number who say they feel a lot of pressure to look good, fit in socially, be involved in extracurricular activities, or be good at sports. The pressures for boys and girls are about the same in each area, although girls are more likely than boys to say they feel a lot of pressure to look good.

A Growing Concern Among Teens

The same 2019 Pew Research Center survey revealed that 96 percent of teens believe that depression and anxiety are a problem among their peers, with 70 percent saying that mental conditions are a "major problem." Mental health tops the list of major problems identified by teens, far ahead of bullying (55 percent), drug addiction (51 percent), and alcohol consumption (45 percent). Juliana Menasce Horowitz and Nikki Graf, authors of the Pew Research Center report, write:

> "Anxiety and depression are on the rise among America's youth and, whether they personally suffer from these conditions or not, seven-in-ten teens today see them as major problems among their peers."[42]
>
> —Juliana Menasce Horowitz and Nikki Graf, analysts with the Pew Research Center

Anxiety and depression are on the rise among America's youth and, whether they personally suffer from these conditions or not, seven-in-ten teens today see them as major problems among their peers. Concern about mental health cuts across gender, racial and socio-economic lines, with roughly equal shares of teens across demographic groups saying it is a significant issue in their community.[42]

There is little doubt that US teenagers are facing more stress, from more sources, than past generations have, and they are struggling to cope with it. Unfortunately, their limited life experience can make it seem like their problems are insurmountable. "I think that life as a teenager is even harder than life as an adult. When you are a teenager, you are feeling things for the first time," says Dese'Rae L. Stage, director of the Live Through This project on suicidal thinking and a two-time suicide survivor herself. "You don't know how you are going to solve that problem, whatever it might be. It doesn't matter what it is, if it makes you feel hopeless, it makes you feel hopeless."[43]

Chapter 4

The People Left Behind

In August 2018 Laura Trujillo traveled from her home in Ohio to the Grand Canyon in northern Arizona with her eleven-year-old daughter, Lucy. Laura wanted her daughter to see the awe-inspiring landforms for herself. Until then, Lucy had known the Grand Canyon only as the place where her grandmother had died. At the time of her mother's death, Laura told Lucy only that her grandmother's heart had stopped working. Four years later, when Lucy was ten, Laura revealed the full truth: Lucy's grandmother had taken her own life, jumping from a rim of the canyon to a stone ledge 100 feet (30 m) below.

Laura Trujillo had also visited the canyon two years earlier, trying to learn everything she could about her mother's suicide. She spoke with a park ranger and with the bus driver who had taken her mother to the scenic overlook where she ended her life. Trujillo's mother had left a notebook on the seat of her car with notes to family members. "Please don't try to find blame. . . . ," she wrote in one. "I have been sick for a very long time and didn't take care of me."[44] But like many suicide survivors, Trujillo did blame herself. Three days before her mother's suicide, Trujillo had sent her mother an email, detailing the sexual abuse she had experienced when she was growing up. "It talked about things that I'd hidden for years, things I was finally trying to make her see," writes Trujillo. "She's gone because she wanted to be gone. But did I push her?"[45]

Survivor's Guilt

Like Trujillo, many suicide survivors feel responsible for the deaths of their loved ones. This is a condition known as survivor's guilt. They often replay the loved one's last days, weeks, months, and years, searching for signs they might have missed and blaming themselves for not doing enough to prevent the suicide. These recurring thoughts can affect the survivor's mental health. A 2016 study by researchers at the University of Kentucky found that suicide survivors—those closest to the suicide—are twice as likely to have diagnosable depression as people who are not exposed to suicide in that way. Survivors were also twice as likely to have diagnosable anxiety. Their odds of having PTSD were about four times higher than for individuals who had not been exposed to suicide.

Laura Trujillo's survivor's guilt sent her into a deep depression. She began to have suicidal thoughts of her own—thoughts she had difficulty sharing with anyone, even her counselor. She writes,

Although Laura Trujillo's mother took her own life by jumping from the rim of the Grand Canyon, Laura eventually came to view the revered natural wonder as a place of beauty and quiet.

"It's a common feeling, this depression after losing someone to suicide, yet it often feels impossible to share. It's raw and scary, and sometimes it feels selfish or indulgent. My mom wasn't a child; she was 66, an adult who made her own decision. And yet it consumed me."[46]

In the years that followed, Trujillo began to realize that she would never fully understand why her mother took her life or if there was anything that could have been done to prevent it. At peace with that knowledge, she took Lucy to the Grand Canyon. "And so I bring my daughter to this place," writes Laura, "not to see where my mom ended her life, not because I think I'll find an answer, but to show her the beauty and the quiet, . . . to witness the grand design of the world, to feel the forces older and stronger than the earth itself, and to accept the vastness of the things we cannot know."[47]

Questioning Everything in Life

The suicide of Marine Corps major John Ruocco left his wife, Kim, so emotionally shattered that she often wished it would all come to a quiet end. "After his death, I cannot say that I was suicidal, but I can remember being in so much emotional pain that I would think, 'I really don't want to wake up,'" Kim says. Nothing made sense to her anymore, and she began to doubt everything about her existence. "My whole world was turned upside down," she says. "What I thought I knew to be true may not have been true. . . . It made me question everything in my life, from my spirituality, to my instincts, to my decision-making, to my marriage, to my family relationships." Kim eventually came to understand that the feelings, doubts, and random thoughts that haunted her daily life were all part of the grieving process. "It's not one feeling, it's a whole bunch of feelings, and I think the advice for anybody who's experiencing grief is that whatever you are feeling, it's OK, it's normal, and it's going to come," she says. "I let it come, I look at it, I feel it, I express it, and then I try to let it go."[48]

Kim Ruocco emerged from the trauma with a renewed sense of purpose in her life. She became involved in suicide prevention and "postvention," a branch of counseling focused on preventing suicide among loss survivors and helping them heal. She became

A Mother Reflects on the Loss of a Son

At 11:15 p.m. on March 10, 2018, police officers in Minnetonka, Minnesota, told Peggy Crandell that her twenty-three-year-old son, Will, had died by suicide. Six months later, Crandell reflected on the loss of her son.

I see my life as two separate pieces. The life I had before my son died, and the life after.

This new life is not easy. It keeps moving forward solely because I wake up in the morning and get out of bed. My feet feel like they are mounted in cement. My heart and chest are heavy. I feel nauseous as if I'm about to make a speech or go bungee jumping. These feelings never go away. They are part of this new life.

My old life is now foreign to me. Even though I remember my son like he was just here at the house visiting, I know I will never get that life back. I am watching it drift away over the horizon. . . .

In one instant, my dreams changed forever. His father and I lost the boy we raised to develop his own life. His sister lost her only sibling— someone who was supposed to be with her to share new life experiences. We only had him with us for 23 years.

People who haven't lost a child try to relate to my experience. Some share what they would do and how they would feel, but they really can't and shouldn't try. . . . I've been told that losing a child is the worst tragedy anyone should have to face. I agree.

Peggy Crandell, "It Begins, Life Without My Son," National Alliance on Mental Illness, September 5, 2018. www.nami.org.

vice president of suicide prevention and postvention at Tragedy Assistance Program for Survivors, a nonprofit organization that provides care and support to families and friends grieving the loss of a member of the armed forces. Ruocco says that she misses her husband every day but that his death taught her to look at the world in a different way. She explains,

> I was more present and connected to the outside world, whether that's nature or other people. I found joy in little things and appreciated little things and moments with people that I may not have discovered prior to my husband's death, and I was able to honor his life lived by telling other people about him and preventing suicide in honor of him.[49]

Feelings of Betrayal

While suicide survivors have experiences in common, each person is different, and so are the thoughts and feelings they ex-

Suicide survivors often find meeting with others who have experienced suicide to be extremely helpful.

perience. Joanne Sosangelis, the director of content operations for Gannett, a media company, lost her partner of fifteen years, Chris, to suicide. She began to attend suicide survivor meetings and found it extremely helpful. But after months of attending the meetings, Sosangelis felt something was different about her experience. She was the only regular participant who had lost a partner; most had lost a child, a sibling, or a parent. "For all that bonded us together, there was something different about those grieving mothers and fathers, brothers and sisters, sons and daughters. Something I sensed but could not quite name,"[50] Sosangelis recalls.

Later, Sosangelis attended a suicide survivors event, where she was seated at a table with other people who had lost partners. As they talked, Sosangelis realized what was different. "Most in my group were wives, some were girlfriends, only one was a husband. But we shared lingering anger, a true sense of betrayal," says Sosangelis. She had felt a similar sense of betrayal when her husband had died of natural causes more than fifteen years before. "But this new anger was different," she says. "It was deeper, more personal, and it was directed squarely at Chris." The betrayal was due in part to the way her partner had ended his life: he had set Sosangelis's house on fire before shooting himself in the bathroom. The sense of betrayal was also a response to how close she had been to partner. "Chris was charming when I met him, supportive. He let me talk about my husband at length. He held me as I shook from crying, even years later," Sosangelis says. "He knew I feared death and abandonment. He knew all of that and still took his life, leaving me with a massive amount of damage to clean up—both physical and emotional."[51]

> "He knew I feared death and abandonment. He knew all of that and still took his life, leaving me with a massive amount of damage to clean up—both physical and emotional."[51]
>
> —Joanne Sosangelis, suicide survivor

Sosangelis has continued to attend the survivor group meetings, seven years after Chris's suicide. It was not something she expected to do. When she first started going to the meetings, people said that they had been coming for ten years or more. "I

A Daughter Forgives Her Mother for Taking Her Life

When writer and florist Melissa Pack was thirty-two, her mother took her life after battling anxiety, depression, and a gambling addiction for years. Pack describes how a superhero movie helped her heal the wounds left by her mother's suicide.

I saw "Wonder Woman" for the first time last summer around the one year anniversary of my mother's suicide. The previous 12 months had been the absolute toughest of my life. I felt utterly defeated in every way ... not only because of my grief, but because the one person in the world who I thought I could count on no matter what let me down in one of the most shocking and excruciatingly painful ways one can. . . .

This new world without my mother felt impossible. It made me question everything I had come to know and count on in the world. . . .

As I watched "Wonder Woman" for the first time, there was something strangely awakening about Diana's story. . . .

Diana learns that accepting the flawed nature of humankind can actually set her free. It enables her to fully embrace her superhero powers, and gives her the solace she needs to continue fighting for good in the world. . . .

What I've realized over time is that my mother may not have been the Wonder Woman I thought she was, but she still had superpowers. Her illness, addiction and suicide didn't define her, nor did it negate the good she put out into the world.

Reimagining my mother as this complex human being—who both struggled and triumphed—has allowed me to begin the process of forgiving her.

Melissa Pack, "When I Realized My Mother Wasn't Wonder Woman," *Mighty* (blog), November 16, 2018. https://themighty.com.

thought, 'No way will I still be coming here that long after.'" But eventually Sosangelis understood why people kept attending. "At some point you go from being the person who needs help to the person who wants to help by sharing your story,"[52] she says.

Honoring Memories

Anger, betrayal, and disappointment are all common emotions among suicide survivors. Karen Ruf, the mother of J.C. Ruf, says she loves her son but hates the choice he made to end his life. "I love J.C., and I always told my kids 'I will love you no matter what you do.' I love him now, and I am not embarrassed of him," she says. "The decision he made? I really hate it. And I would ground him for it, if he were here," she says, using dark humor to alleviate the pain. "He would not be on the X-Box for a month—at least."[53]

The pain of J.C.'s death is so great that Karen has to make a conscious effort to get out of bed each morning. "Every single day, when I open my eyes, I have a choice to make," she says. "And I make a choice to get up and do what I can with that day— go to work, and surround myself with people who love me, who love J.C."[54] That includes spending time with his baseball team. When J.C. was alive, Karen attended every game, even when he was not scheduled to pitch. The spring after J.C.'s suicide, when baseball season began, the baseball coach, Tom Daria, kept J.C.'s name on the Dixie Heights High School team roster, and the team wore J.C.'s number on their uniforms. And there in the stands was Karen Ruf.

Allie Doss comforts herself after the loss of her sixteen-year-old daughter, Sara Prideaux, by keeping her daughter's room just as she left it three years ago. The purse and camera Sara took to Spain when she spent a summer abroad still hang on a closet doorknob. The teen's favorite stuffed animals hang in a net over the bed. "I'm sure they're dusty, but no one is allowed to touch them," says Doss. Sara's favorite comforter is on the bed. Doss washes it regularly. "The first year after she passed I would come in here and just lose it and be angry and resentful and sad," Doss remembers. Three years after her daughter's suicide, Doss still struggles with her grief. She feels like Sara's suicide was an act of rejection and that she must have been a bad parent. But she feels closer to her daughter when she visits her room. "This is her museum," says Doss. "I can look at anything, and I know that she touched that, she touched that. So now it's my place of solace."[55]

Writing about their feelings is another way that suicide survivors can feel close to the loved ones they have lost and help deal with their grief. Debbie Baird is among those who found writing to be therapeutic. When her twenty-nine-year-old son, Matthew, took his life, Debbie was sure her grief would never subside. She went to counseling, joined a support group, and began writing in a journal. She found that writing down her secret thoughts and emotions helped her heal. "I kept thinking if I could write a letter to him, maybe he'd write back to me. Maybe he'd let me know the reason why this happened. I felt like I needed to find a way to connect with him," she says. Slowly, she saw a change in what she wrote. "It went from wanting to know why, and how hurt and sad I felt and how my heart was broken and all my physical pain that I was going through and my depression and how I was feeling to, 'Hey, [Matt's sister] Jen's going to have another baby.' I could see my life changing."[56]

Grieving the Youngest Suicides

The loss of any loved one is painful, but the loss of a child is especially devastating, in part because youngsters have their entire lives ahead of them. When they die, their future—everything they might accomplish and all the love they might feel—dies with them. When the death is the result of a suicide, the loss is magnified, in part because suicide usually is the result of a feeling of hopelessness that it is hard to imagine a child having. Nevertheless, the CDC reports that from 1999 to 2016 the number of suicides among children younger than age twelve increased

Researchers have found that among children, bullying is a major factor in suicides.

70 percent. A 2016 study by researchers from Nationwide Children's Hospital in Columbus, Ohio, found that depression did not appear to be a major factor in child suicides but that bullying did.

This was the case in the suicide of nine-year-old Madison Whitsett, who attempted to take her life on November 9, 2018, and died from the injuries three days later. "I was there from the day she was born to the day they took her off the machine," says her father, James Whitsett. "It's very hard to watch your child flatline. There ain't nothing you can do. The only thing I knew to do was to be there and pray and hold her, and that's what I did."[57] Madison had struggled with attention-deficit/hyperactivity disorder. This appears to have made her a target for bullies, who called her "stupid" and "dumb."

Like most suicide survivors, James Whitsett wonders if he could have done anything to prevent his daughter's death. "I'm still trying to get answers," he says. "Every day. There ain't a day don't go by, or minute, that I don't just sit and try to rewind things. What could I have done? What did I miss, if I missed anything?"[58]

> "There ain't a day don't go by, or minute, that I don't just sit and try to rewind things. What could I have done? What did I miss, if I missed anything?"[58]
>
> —James Whitsett, suicide survivor

And so the ripples of self-doubt, survivor's guilt, and depression continue to spread, encompassing the lives of thousands more survivors each week. Some survivors dedicate their lives to helping others avoid the fate of the loved one they lost. Others write books, poems, and articles, to express their pain and perhaps awaken others to be more involved in the lives of those around them. And others simply do their best to get through each day, coping with their grief and remembering those who left them behind.

Chapter 5

What Can Be Done to Prevent Suicide?

Suicide is a leading cause of preventable death in the United States. A preventable death is a premature death that could have been avoided with proper medical intervention. An increase in preventable deaths is the main reason that life expectancy in the United States has dropped for the first time in decades, according to a 2018 CDC report. "Tragically, this troubling trend is largely driven by deaths from drug overdose and suicide," said Robert R. Redfield, director of the CDC. "These sobering statistics are a wake-up call that we are losing too many Americans, too early and too often, to conditions that are preventable."[59]

Challenges to Suicide Prevention

The idea of suicide prevention is not new. In 1968 Edwin S. Shneidman founded the American Association of Suicidology, a nonprofit organization devoted to suicide prevention and support of those affected by it. Other suicide prevention organizations followed, including the American Foundation for Suicide Prevention, founded in 1987. In 1992 Congress established the Substance Abuse and Mental Health Services Administration (SAMHSA), a branch of the US Department of Health and Human Services. SAMHSA helped create a suicide prevention network of 161 crisis centers that provides a toll-free hotline available to anyone in suicidal crisis or emotional distress. For many years these suicide prevention efforts seemed to be paying off. The rate of suicide fell from a high of 12.99 per 100,000 population in 1986 to a low of 10.4 in 2000. Since 2000, however, the suicide rate has steadily increased, reaching 14.0 per 100,000 in 2017—a 35 percent increase.

Part of the reason for the rise in suicide is demographics. The US population is getting older, and older people are more likely to take their lives than younger people are. This is especially true in the oldest group. Those over age sixty-five have a suicide rate of about 18 per 100,000, which is 28 percent higher than the national average. And the over-sixty-five population is growing faster than any other age group. In 1950 just 8 percent of Americans were over sixty-five. By 2017 that number had nearly doubled to 15.7 percent of the population. People in this age group face declining health, lack of purpose related to jobs and careers, and

Adults over the age of sixty-five have a suicide rate 28 percent higher than the national average.

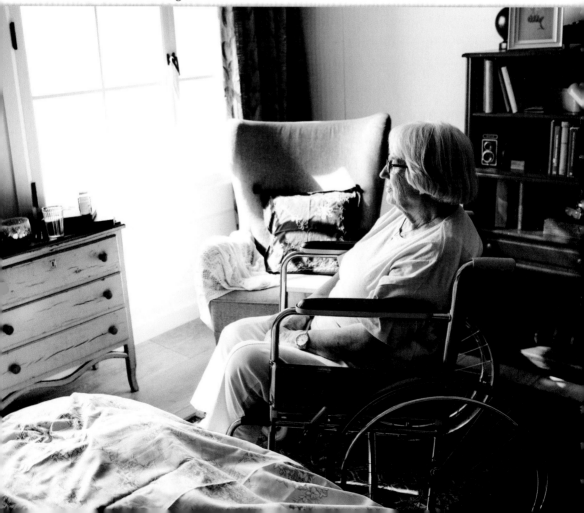

the loss of spouses due to natural causes. Many believe their best years are behind them, and they have little to look forward to. In addition, a growing number no longer view suicide as taboo. A 2018 study by Yi Tong of the City University of New York and Julie Phillips of Rutgers University found that the percentage of US adults who said suicide is acceptable in the case of incurable disease increased from 46.9 percent to 61.4 percent from the 1980s to the 2010s. The percentage that said suicide is acceptable if a person is "tired of living" rose from 13.7 to 19.1 percent.

The growing acceptance of suicide among the elderly is due in part to the "death with dignity" movement, which argues that terminally ill people have a right to take their own lives, and doctors should be free to assist them. As a result, several states have adopted doctor-assisted suicide laws. Tong and Phillips say that because of these laws "the act [of suicide] has become somewhat normalized, contributing to more accepting attitudes,"[60] even when people are not terminally ill. Reversing the tide of this acceptance of suicide is extremely difficult. It is not a matter of education. Tong and Phillips found that acceptance of suicide is greatest among the most highly educated. Tom Jacobs, a senior staff writer at the online publication the *Pacific Standard*, looks at Tong and Phillips's research another way. He believes that the greater acceptance of suicide has a hopeful side. "The findings are a reminder that the stigma around suicide remains strong," he writes. "If it continues to decline, Americans may become more willing to talk about, and get counseling for, their suicidal thoughts— which would ultimately lead to fewer tragic deaths."[61]

> "The act [of suicide] has become somewhat normalized, contributing to more accepting attitudes."[60]
>
> —Yi Tong and Julie Phillips, public health researchers

Breaking the Silence

Many people are not comfortable talking about suicide. Sometimes people think that if they bring up the topic, the people they are talking to will start to think about doing it. As a result, suicide is not discussed as much as it should be, considering how many lives it claims each year. "It sounds weird to say we want to talk about suicide all the time," says John Ackerman, suicide prevention coordinator at Nationwide Children's Hospital and the Center for Suicide Prevention and Research. "But that is healthy, [and] absolutely a child is less at risk if they don't feel like it's a shut door."[62]

> "It sounds weird to say we want to talk about suicide all the time. But that is healthy, [and] absolutely a child is less at risk if they don't feel like it's a shut door."[62]
>
> —John Ackerman, suicide prevention coordinator at Nationwide Children's Hospital and the Center for Suicide Prevention and Research

What is true for children and adolescents is also true for adults: discussing suicide will reduce the stigma, making it easier for individuals who are thinking about suicide to share their feelings. That is why the first step in the National Institute of Mental Health's (NIMH) "5 Action Steps for Helping Someone in Emotional Pain" is "Ask: 'Are you thinking about killing yourself?'" The experts at the NIMH insist that asking this question will not be harmful. "Studies show that asking at-risk individuals if they are suicidal does not increase suicides or suicidal thoughts," says the NIMH. "Acknowledging and talking about suicide may in fact reduce rather than increase suicidal thoughts."[63]

Asking about suicide and discussing it does not guarantee that the person at risk will be deterred. Those who are most intent on taking their own lives realize that if they tell another person about their suicidal thoughts, that person will try to stop them from carrying out their plans. "The paradox is that the people who are most intent on committing suicide know that they have to keep their plans to themselves if they are to carry out the act," says Michael Miller, an assistant professor of psychiatry at Harvard Medical School. "Thus, the people most in need of help may be the toughest to save."[64]

Researchers at Columbia University are working on ways to penetrate the shroud of secrecy that surrounds suicidal thinking. They have developed a suicide risk assessment tool known as the Columbia-Suicide Severity Rating Scale (C-SSRS), or the Columbia Protocol, to identify whether someone is at risk for suicide, assess the severity and immediacy of that risk, and gauge the level of support that the person needs.

Preventing Suicide with Cell Phone Apps

One of the biggest challenges in suicide prevention is getting at-risk individuals to discuss their suicidal thoughts or mental health problems. Suicide prevention professionals have developed cell phone apps as a way to allow at-risk individuals to obtain help without having to speak to a counselor about their thoughts and feelings. Several mental health and suicide prevention apps are now available, including Stay Alive, LifeLine, R U Suicidal?, DMHS Suicide Prevention App, and Operation Life. Most of the apps provide a list of warning signs that the user can check to see whether he or she is at risk.

The DMHS Suicide Prevention App includes an interactive self-test featuring a chatbot, a computer program designed to simulate conversation with human users. The chatbot asks various questions as if chatting via text. Depending on the user's replies, the chatbot will suggest steps for the user to take. The app lets the user create a safety plan to follow if he or she is feeling suicidal.

A team of Spanish researchers reviewed existing mental health apps and found the concept promising. "Based on our experience in clinical and real cases, we conclude that mHealth [mental health] apps are an essential tool that can help us to prevent suicide, considering the family, caregivers, and health professionals that are part of helping to save a life through the use of ICTs [information and communications technologies]," they write. "Saving even a single life via a mobile app is a breakthrough."

Isabel de la Torre et al., "Mobile Apps for Suicide Prevention: Review of Virtual Stores and Literature," *JMIR mHealth and uHealth*, October 2017. www.ncbi.nlm.nih.gov.

The C-SSRS questions have been repeatedly tested under scientific conditions and found to elicit honest and clear responses. Most importantly, the test employs simple language so it can be used by people who are not medical professionals. Kelly Posner, a clinical professor in the Department of Child and Adolescent Psychiatry at Columbia University and one of the developers of the C-SSRS, explains:

> Anyone can use this life-saving tool. We have worked with every type of organization—the military; veterans; schools, colleges and universities; health care institutions; first responders; and many government agencies and have witnessed the dramatic impact on suicide rates where talking openly about suicide has been embraced and these helpful simple questions are put in everyone's hands.[65]

The C-SSRS's effectiveness has been documented in several studies. For example, the US Marine Corps began using it in 2014, putting it in the hands of support staff, including legal assistants, financial aid counselors, and clergy. In three years the tool contributed to a 3.5 percent reduction in suicides. On the basis of those results, the US Department of Defense has rolled out the program for use by nonmedical personnel in the other branches of the armed forces. After its adoption by Tennessee-based Centerstone, a nonprofit provider of behavioral health care to more than 170,000 patients a year in five states, the C-SSRS has helped reduce the suicide rate among its patients from 31 suicides per 100,000 population to 11 suicides per 100,000 in just twenty months.

Medical Interventions

The American Medical Association (AMA), the largest association of physicians and medical students in the United States, agrees that more questions have to be asked of at-risk indi-

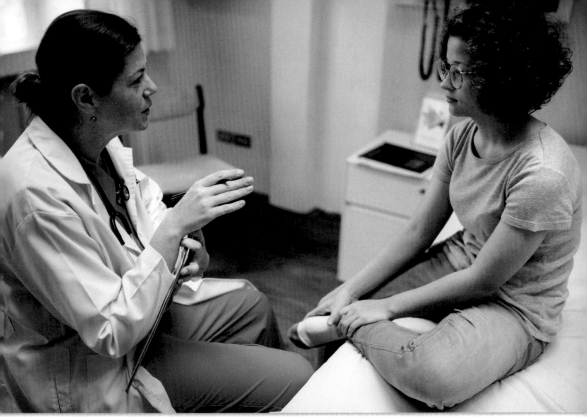

The American Medical Association is calling for additional training for doctors to help them assess suicide risk in their patients and conduct safety counseling.

viduals. In June 2018 the AMA adopted a new policy calling for additional training for physicians to help them assess suicide risk and conduct safety counseling. This is important, because doctors are ideally situated to conduct such screening. In approximately 75 percent of completed suicides, the individuals had seen a physician within the year before their death. In 45 to 66 percent of the cases, the doctor visits occurred within a month of the suicide.

Many of those medical visits are related to suicidal thoughts. Patients with these thoughts make up the most at-risk population. A 2017 study of patients who are discharged from hospitals after being admitted because of suicidal thoughts found that the suicide rate for these individuals was 484 per 100,000 population. That rate is thirty-five times higher than the overall US national suicide rate. Suicide prevention experts believe that closer follow-up of these discharged patients could save many lives.

Focusing on Means

Risk assessments based on asking questions can be effective with individuals who are thinking about suicide, but not everyone who takes his or her life has been planning to do so. For example, minutes before taking his life on New Year's Eve 2018, fifteen-year-old Devin Hodges was not considering suicide. Only after accidentally shooting his friend did Hodges think of taking his own life. The only reason he could carry out the act was that he had the means to do so—a loaded gun in his hand. If he did not have the gun, or if it was not loaded, chances are Hodges would be alive today. This is the thinking behind the "means matters" approach to suicide prevention. Advocates of this kind of intervention believe that reducing access to suicide tools is an important facet of suicide prevention.

The means matters approach grew out of events that occurred in the United Kingdom. For generations, the British used a flammable gas made from coal, known as coal gas, to heat their homes and cook their food. Coal gas can be deadly when inhaled, because it contains the lethal gas carbon monoxide. As a result, a suicidal person could take his or her life by opening the valve to a coal gas oven and breathing the fumes. In the 1950s twenty-five hundred people a year killed themselves in coal gas ovens. However, when Great Britain switched over to using natural gas, which contains almost no carbon monoxide, the number of suicides dropped by one-third. Without a means of suicide at hand, fewer people took their lives.

The same thinking is behind the construction of suicide barriers on bridges. For example, from 1979 to 1985, twenty-one people took their lives by jumping from the Duke Ellington Bridge in Washington, DC, which stands 125 feet (38 m) above Rock Creek Park. Meanwhile, the nearby Taft Bridge, which is a similar height but has a higher barrier wall, had fewer than fourteen suicides during the same period. Experts believed that if a suicide barrier was built on the Ellington Bridge, suicidal people would simply use the Taft Bridge, but that is not what happened. Five

Experts believe that building higher barriers on bridges is one way of reducing suicides.

years after suicide barriers were installed on the Ellington Bridge, a study found that suicides on the bridge were eliminated completely, but the number on the Taft Bridge barely changed.

Means matters advocates in the United States focus their efforts on guns, which are involved in about half of all US suicides. A 2005 study of 153 survivors of suicide attempts, aged thirteen to thirty-four, found that 87 percent of the survivors made their suicide attempt within eight hours of deciding to complete the suicide, and about half (48 percent) made the attempt within less than twenty minutes. If an individual survives a suicide attempt, the crisis usually passes, and in the vast majority of cases—93 percent, according to the Harvard T.H. Chan School of Public Health—the person does not end up dying by suicide at a later date. Means matters advocates want to close that window of opportunity when a suicidal person is most at risk by requiring gun owners to lock up their firearms.

Currently only one state, Massachusetts, requires that all firearms be stored in a locked container or equipped with a tamper-resistant mechanical lock or other safety device. Three other states—California, Connecticut, and New York—require such devices only when the gun owner lives with a person who is not allowed by federal law to possess a gun, such as a convicted felon. Means matters advocates believe that requiring gun owners in every state to keep their weapons under lock and key would reduce suicides significantly, especially among the young. According to a 2015 study by the Brady Center to Prevent Gun

The Columbia Protocol for Risk Assessment

The Columbia-Suicide Severity Rating Scale (C-SSRS), or Columbia Protocol, is a questionnaire designed to detect and rate a person's risk of suicide. It is designed to discover whether a person has thought about suicide (ideation), what actions—if any—the person has taken to prepare for suicide, and if he or she began a suicide attempt that was either interrupted by another person or stopped of his or her own volition. Although intended for use by a wide range of people, the test can be administered only by a person trained in its use. Some of the questions include:

1. Have you wished you were dead or wished you could go to sleep and not wake up?
2. Have you actually had thoughts of killing yourself?
3. Have you been thinking about how you might kill yourself?
4. Have you had these thoughts and had some intention of acting on them?
5. Have you started to work out or worked out the details of how to kill yourself?
6. Have you ever done anything, started to do anything, or prepared to do anything to end your life?
6a. Was this within the last year?

Duke University Health System, "C-SSRS (Columbia-Suicide Severity Rating Scale)," 2018. https://sites .duke.edu.

Violence, 82 percent of teen firearm suicides involve a family member's gun.

Daniel W. Webster, director of the Center for Gun Policy and Research at Johns Hopkins University, believes that what is needed is a change in attitude regarding the availability of guns to those who might be suicidal. Webster explains:

> One thing that many people in public health are beginning to talk about is . . . holding firearms from individuals when they're going through some crisis that might elevate their risk for suicide. So just as a friend or family member, as a caring thing to do about someone's safety, would say, "Let me get you, let me drive you home because you've had too much to drink," you do the same thing with saying, "Let me hold your guns while you're going through this divorce. Let me keep your guns after you just lost your job and are very distraught."[66]

Several cultural forces are contributing to the suicide epidemic in the United States, including an aging population, a growing acceptance of suicide, a large number of veterans returning from war, and a tendency for people to connect via social media rather than in person. Doctors, nurses, counselors, teachers, friends, and family must all learn the warning signs of suicide and be vigilant in watching for it. "Suicide can be prevented—which sets it apart from other sources of pain and suffering in the world," says Posner. "We need to get to a place where everybody, everywhere asks the questions that help identify at-risk individuals and get them the help that they need. Together, we can prevent these unnecessary tragedies."[67]

"Suicide can be prevented—which sets it apart from other sources of pain and suffering in the world."[67]

—Kelly Posner, a clinical professor in the Department of Child and Adolescent Psychiatry at Columbia University

Introduction: The Recent Surge in Suicides

1. Anne Schuchat, "Transcript for VitalSigns Teleconference: Suicide Prevention," Centers for Disease Control and Prevention, June 7, 2018. www.cdc.gov.
2. Deb Stone et al., *Preventing Suicide: A Technical Package of Policy, Programs, and Practices*. Atlanta: National Center for Injury Prevention and Control, Centers for Disease Control and Prevention, 2017, p. 7.
3. Lighthouse Project (@C_SSRS), "Suicide takes more firemen," Twitter, February 15, 2019, 11:51 a.m. https://twitter.com.
4. Schuchat, "Transcript for VitalSigns Teleconference."

Chapter One: A Disturbing Trend

5. Quoted in Molly Knight, "Solomon Thomas: My Sister 'Was the Light of My Life,'" ESPN, September 19, 2018. http://tv5.espn.com.
6. Quoted in Knight, "Solomon Thomas."
7. Danny O'Neel, "I Survived Combat in Iraq and a Suicide Attempt at Home. But Many Veterans Aren't So Lucky," *USA Today*, January 16, 2019. www.usatoday.com.
8. O'Neel, "I Survived Combat in Iraq and a Suicide Attempt at Home."
9. Quoted in Alia E. Dastagir, "Suicide Never Entered His Mind. Then 9/11 Happened," *USA Today*, December 26, 2018. www.usatoday.com.
10. Quoted in Centers for Disease Control and Prevention, "Suicide Increasing Among American Workers," November 15, 2018. www.cdc.gov.
11. Quoted in Centers for Disease Control and Prevention, "New Study Finds Higher than Expected Number of Suicide Deaths Among U.S. Veterinarians," December 20, 2018. www.cdc.gov.

12. Kate Harding, "I Went on a Walk and Returned to Find My Husband Dead," *Guardian* (Manchester), February 24, 2018. www.theguardian.com.

13. Quoted in Harding, "I Went on a Walk and Returned to Find My Husband Dead."

14. Harding, "I Went on a Walk and Returned to Find My Husband Dead."

15. Michelle M. Johns et al., "Transgender Identity and Experiences of Violence Victimization, Substance Use, Suicide Risk, and Sexual Risk Behaviors Among High School Students—19 States and Large Urban School Districts, 2017," Centers for Disease Control and Prevention, January 25, 2019. www.cdc.gov.

16. Quoted in Joseph Bednar, "Suicide Rates Continue to Rise; the Question Is Why," BusinessWest.com, August 20, 2018. https://businesswest.com.

Chapter Two: The Causes of Suicide

17. "What Is Mental Illness?," American Psychiatric Association, August 2018. www.psychiatry.org.

18. Quoted in Locke Hughes, "What Everyone Needs to Know About the Rising U.S. Suicide Rates," *Shape*, June 14, 2018. www.shape.com.

19. Suicide Awareness Voices of Education, "Depression," 2019. https://save.org.

20. M.K. Nock et al., "Mental Disorders, Comorbidity and Suicidal Behavior: Results from the National Comorbidity Survey Replication," *Molecular Psychiatry*, 2010. www.ncbi.nlm.nih.gov.

21. Quoted in April Dembosky, "She Wanted to Be the Perfect Mom, Then Landed in a Psychiatric Unit," WBUR News (Boston), January 19, 2019. www.wbur.org.

22. Quoted in Dembosky, "She Wanted to Be the Perfect Mom, Then Landed in a Psychiatric Unit."

23. Roy B. Sessions, "Suicide in Cancer Patients," *Cancer Experience* (blog), *Psychology Today*, August 26, 2016. www.psychologytoday.com.

24. Quoted in Fiza Pirani, "Suicide Risk 4 Times Worse for Cancer Patients, Study Finds—What Clinicians Can Do to Help," *Atlanta Journal-Constitution*, January 14, 2019. www.ajc.com.

25. Mikael Rostila, Jan Saarela, and Ichiro Kawachi, "Suicide Following the Death of a Sibling: A Nationwide Follow-up Study from Sweden," *BMJ Open*, April 26, 2013. https://bmjopen.bmj.com.

26. Rostila, Saarela, and Kawachi, "Suicide Following the Death of a Sibling."

27. Quoted in Jessica Boddy, "The Forces Driving Middle-Aged White People's 'Deaths of Despair,'" National Public Radio, March 23, 2017. www.npr.org.

Chapter Three: Teen Suicide

28. Quoted in Anne Saker, "Crestview Hills Teen's Suicide Leaves Family Trying to Understand What Happened," Cincinnati.com, December 28, 2017. www.cincinnati.com.

29. Quoted in Saker, "Crestview Hills Teen's Suicide Leaves Family Trying to Understand What Happened."

30. Quoted in Saker, "Crestview Hills Teen's Suicide Leaves Family Trying to Understand What Happened."

31. Quoted in Rae Daniel, "CDC: Suicide Rates Increased 70 Percent Among Youth from 2006 to 2016," WCPO News, March 21, 2018. www.wcpo.com.

32. Quoted in Jayne O'Donnell and Anne Saker, "Teen Suicide Is Soaring. Do Spotty Mental Health and Addiction Treatment Share Blame?," *USA Today*, March 19, 2018. www.usatoday.com.

33. Farid Naib, "Cayman's Story," YouTube, September 8, 2015. https://youtu.be/taUfarsaZYo.

34. Quoted in Perri Klass, "Kids' Suicide-Related Hospital Visits Rise Sharply," *New York Times*, May 16, 2018. www.nytimes.com.

35. Quoted in Maggie Fox, "More Teens Are Attempting Suicide. It's Not Clear Why," NBC News, May 16, 2018. www.nbcnews.com.

36. Quoted in Sabrina Tavernise, "Young Adolescents as Likely to Die from Suicide as from Traffic Accidents," *New York Times*, November 3, 2016. www.nytimes.com.

37. Quoted in Tavernise, "Young Adolescents as Likely to Die from Suicide as from Traffic Accidents."

38. Quoted in Sonya Collins, "Teen Suicide: 'The Time for Secrecy Is Over,'" WebMD, July 25, 2017. www.webmd.com.

39. Quoted in Madalyn Mendoza, "Alamo Heights Student Was a Victim of Bullying Before Committing Suicide, Family Says," mySA, January 8, 2016. www.mysanantonio.com.

40. Quoted in Mendoza, "Alamo Heights Student Was a Victim of Bullying Before Committing Suicide, Family Says."

41. Quoted in Saker, "Crestview Hills Teen's Suicide Leaves Family Trying to Understand What Happened."

42. Juliana Menasce Horowitz and Nikki Graf, "Most U.S. Teens See Anxiety and Depression as a Major Problem Among Their Peers," Pew Research Center, February 20, 2019. www.pewsocialtrends.org.

43. Quoted in Fox, "More Teens Are Attempting Suicide."

Chapter Four: The People Left Behind

44. Quoted in Laura Trujillo, "Stepping Back from the Edge," *USA Today*, November 29, 2018. www.usatoday.com.

45. Trujillo, "Stepping Back from the Edge."

46. Trujillo, "Stepping Back from the Edge."

47. Trujillo, "Stepping Back from the Edge."

48. Quoted in Alia E. Dastagir, "After a Suicide, Here's What Happens to the People Left Behind," *USA Today*, December 17, 2018. www.usatoday.com.

49. Quoted in Dastagir, "After a Suicide, Here's What Happens to the People Left Behind."

50. Joanne Sosangelis, "My Partner Died by Suicide. He Doesn't Know the Damage He Left Behind," *USA Today*, December 17, 2018. www.usatoday.com.

51. Sosangelis, "My Partner Died by Suicide."

52. Sosangelis, "My Partner Died by Suicide."

53. Quoted in Saker, "Crestview Hills Teen's Suicide Leaves Family Trying to Understand What Happened."

54. Quoted in Saker, "Crestview Hills Teen's Suicide Leaves Family Trying to Understand What Happened."

55. Quoted in Laura Ziegler, "With Teen Suicide on the Rise in Kansas City, Adults Ask Young People What They Need," KCUR 89.3 (Kansas City, MO), December 20, 2018. www.kcur.org.

56. Quoted in Dastagir, "After a Suicide, Here's What Happens to the People Left Behind."

57. Quoted in Sarah Verser, "'I Miss My Baby,' AL Father on the Pain of Losing Young Daughter to Suicide," WBRC Fox 6 News (Birmingham, AL), February 28, 2019. www.wbrc.com.

58. Quoted in Verser, "'I Miss My Baby,' AL Father on the Pain of Losing Young Daughter to Suicide."

Chapter Five: What Can Be Done to Prevent Suicide?

59. Robert R. Redfield, "CDC Director's Media Statement on U.S. Life Expectancy," Centers for Disease Control and Prevention, November 29, 2018. www.cdc.gov.

60. Quoted in Tom Jacobs, "Americans' Attitudes Toward Suicide Are Softening," *Pacific Standard*, September 21, 2018. https://psmag.com.

61. Jacobs, "Americans' Attitudes Toward Suicide Are Softening."

62. Quoted in Ziegler, "With Teen Suicide on the Rise in Kansas City, Adults Ask Young People What They Need."

63. National Institute of Mental Health, "Suicide Prevention," March 2017. www.nimh.nih.gov.

64. Quoted in Patrick J. Skerrett, "Suicide Often Not Preceded by Warnings," *Harvard Health Blog*, Harvard Medical School, October 29, 2015. www.health.harvard.edu.

65. Kelly Posner, "Preventing Suicide: Teen Deaths Are on the Rise, but We Know How to Fight Back," *USA Today*, February 7, 2018. www.usatoday.com.

66. Quoted in Elena Guobyte et al., "Global Mortality from Firearms, 1990–2016," YouTube, August 28, 2018. www.youtube.com/watch?v=VucFxSkbDwY

67. Posner, "Preventing Suicide."

Warning Signs

The National Suicide Prevention Lifeline lists common warning signs that might help you determine whether a friend or loved one is at risk for suicide. These signs might be especially important if the behavior is new, has increased, or seems related to a painful event, loss, or change.

- Talking about wanting to die or to kill themselves
- Looking for a way to kill themselves, like searching online or buying a gun
- Talking about feeling hopeless or having no reason to live
- Talking about feeling trapped or in unbearable pain
- Talking about being a burden to others
- Increasing the use of alcohol or drugs
- Acting anxious or agitated; behaving recklessly
- Sleeping too little or too much
- Withdrawing or isolating themselves
- Showing rage or talking about seeking revenge
- Extreme mood swings

National Suicide Prevention Lifeline, "We Can All Prevent Suicide." https://suicidepreventionlifeline.org.

If you or someone you know exhibits any of these signs, seek help by calling the National Suicide Prevention Lifeline at 800-273-8255.

Organizations to Contact

Alliance of Hope for Suicide Loss Survivors
website: www.allianceofhope.org

Alliance of Hope for Suicide Loss Survivors is a nonprofit organization that provides information to help survivors understand the complex emotional aftermath of suicide. Its website features a blog, bookstore, and memorials.

American Association of Suicidology (AAS)
5221 Wisconsin Ave. NW
Washington, DC 20015
website: www.suicidology.org

Founded in 1968 by Edwin S. Shneidman, the AAS promotes research, public awareness programs, public education, and training for professionals and volunteers. In addition, the AAS serves as a national clearinghouse for information on suicide. Its mission is to promote the understanding and prevention of suicide and support those who have been affected by it.

American Foundation for Suicide Prevention (AFSP)
120 Wall St., Twenty-Ninth Floor
New York, NY 10005
website: www.afsp.org

Established in 1987, the AFSP is dedicated to saving lives and bringing hope to those affected by suicide. It offers those affected by suicide a nationwide community and supports them through education, advocacy, and research.

Centre for Suicide Prevention
105 Twelfth Ave. SE, Suite 320
Calgary, AB, Canada T2G 1A1
website: www.suicideinfo.ca

Established in 1981, the Centre for Suicide Prevention is a non-profit organization that is a branch of the Canadian Mental Health Association. Its mission is to educate people with the information, knowledge, and skills necessary to respond to people at risk of suicide.

Jason Foundation
18 Volunteer Dr.
Hendersonville, TN 37075
website: www.jasonfoundation.com

The Jason Foundation provides curriculum material to schools, parents, and other teens about how teen suicide can be prevented. It is dedicated to the prevention of the silent epidemic of youth suicide through educational and awareness programs that equip young people, educators, youth workers, and parents with the tools and resources to help identify and assist at-risk youth.

Sibling Survivors of Suicide Loss
website: www.siblingsurvivors.com

The Sibling Survivors of Suicide Loss site aims to provide a safe place for anyone who has lost a sister or brother to suicide. It is a place for people who have lost a sibling to suicide to share memories, discuss their feelings and experiences, and share photos. It is also a place to connect with others who have lost a sister or brother to suicide.

The Trevor Project
PO Box 69232
West Hollywood, CA 90069
website: www.thetrevorproject.org

Founded in 1998 by the creators of the Academy Award–winning short film *Trevor*, the Trevor Project is a national organization providing crisis intervention and suicide prevention services to LGBTQ young people aged thirteen to twenty-four.

For Further Research

Books

Amy Bleuel, *Project Semicolon: Your Story Isn't Over*. New York: HarperCollins, 2017.

Cherese Cartlidge, *Teens and Suicide*. San Diego: ReferencePoint, 2017.

Keith Jones, *Suicide Information for Teens*. Detroit: Omnigraphics, 2017.

Bradley Steffens, *Thinking Critically: Teen Suicide*. San Diego: ReferencePoint, 2019.

Jean M. Twenge, *iGen: Why Today's Super-connected Kids Are Growing Up Less Rebellious, More Tolerant, Less Happy—and Completely Unprepared for Adulthood*. New York: Atria, 2017.

Internet Sources

Alia E. Dastagir, "Suicide Never Entered His Mind. Then 9/11 Happened," *USA Today*, December 26, 2018. www.usatoday.com.

Molly Knight, "Solomon Thomas: My Sister 'Was the Light of My Life,'" ESPN, September 19, 2018. http://tv5.espn.com.

National Institute of Mental Health, "Antidepressant Medications for Children and Adolescents: Information for Parents and Caregivers," National Institutes of Health. www.nimh.nih.gov.

Danny O'Neel, "I Survived Combat in Iraq and a Suicide Attempt at Home. But Many Veterans Aren't So Lucky," *USA Today*, January 16, 2019. www.usatoday.com.

Sabrina Tavernise, "Young Adolescents as Likely to Die from Suicide as from Traffic Accidents," *New York Times*, November 3, 2016. www.nytimes.com.

Laura Trujillo, "Stepping Back from the Edge," *USA Today*, November 29, 2018. www.usatoday.com.

Picture Credits

Cover: B-D-S Piotr Marcinski

  5: Associated Press
11: Cpl D Morgan/USMC/ZUMA Press/Newscom
13: FatCamera/iStock.com
16: kali9/iStock.com
21: Alfred Pasieka/Science Photo Library/Alfred Pasieka/SPL/
     Newscom
25: Maury Aaseng
27: Jacob Lund/Shutterstock.com
31: pixelheadphoto/iStock.com
35: SolStock/iStock.com
38: Edward A. Ornelas/ZUMA Press/Newscom
43: miroslav_1/iStock.com
46: shironosov/iStock.com
51: HighwayStarz-Photography/iStock.com
54, 59: Rawpixel/iStock.com
61: Johnrob/iStock.com

About the Author

Bradley Steffens is a poet, a novelist, and an award-winning author of more than fifty nonfiction books for children and young adults. He is also a suicide survivor. His thirty-three-year-old son Ezekiel took his life in July 2014. This book is dedicated to his memory.